To:

....

A joy encountered simply for a moment,
An ache that will persist a lifetime,
A love that will endure for eternity.

Every life is beautiful...

From:

....

Date: ....

Christ's Passion

Hope and comfort through miscarriage

HEIDE L. WRIGHT

Ark House Press
arkhousepress.com

© 2023 Heide L. Wright

All rights reserved, including the right to reproduce this book, or portions thereof in any form whatsoever.

Cataloguing in Publication Data:
Title: Christ's Passion
ISBN: 978-0-6459207-4-1 (pbk.) 978-0-6459938-5-1 (hdbk.)
Subjects: FAM059000 [FAMILY & RELATIONSHIPS / Miscarriage & Baby Loss] REL012010 [RELIGION / Christian Living / Death, Grief, Bereavement]; REL012040 [RELIGION / Christian Living / Inspirational];

References
Ney, Dr. Philip G. 1997, *Deeply Damaged*, Pioneer Publishing Co. Ltd. Canada, p.144-146.

Scripture quotations taken from the (NASB®) New American Standard Bible®, Copyright © 1960, 1971, 1977, 1995, 2020 by The Lockman Foundation. Used by permission. All rights reserved. lockman.org

For

HOLLY GRACE, MALACIAH FAITH
AND CAROLINE ROSE.

*"I'll love you forever, in my heart it's
you I hold. Your lives have a mighty
purpose, through your story told."*

She waits for me...

Glorious ray of sunshine,
Subtle *Mountain Dew*,
A warm gentle evening breeze,
Drawing me closer to you.

The roaring of the thunder,
The change in something sweet,
An over ripeness of colour,
The orchestra made to take a seat.

The acoustics of a season changing,
Come back my *Mountain Dew*,
A stain made through a misty haze,
A deep longing for that I knew.

A time to toil; a time to rest,
Take in the breath of wonder,
Watch for ladybugs; imagine them dance,
Peacefully dream as you enjoy their trance.

Through the *Mountain Dew*,
I see a lustre in the sky,
Fruition of months coming together,
A glimmer of perfection passes by.

The calming of the ocean,
A beauty arises as the sunsets,
I hold onto the special blessings that do,
Remind me oh so much of you...

You are a precious gift, one that waits for me,
I love you *Mountain Dew*...

I feel so alone... Life continues around me, however in my being, time is motionless. The world is advancing and doesn't even pause to recognise that I've lost my baby. Still here am I, sitting in this frozen reality concealing a pain so deep, it shatters my soul into a million pieces. I cry out in brokenness as I carry an incoherent fear of there being no means of escape from this grave dissolution. To make matters worse, those around me don't know what to say, so to not cause me further impairment, they remain silent. They love me yet not acknowledging my child forces me into yet a greater form of loneliness. Why are people unable to recognise that a baby who dies in the womb, is as certain a human being as anyone else in this world?

It's one of those harrowing times that you can only sincerely comprehend having personally experienced it. There are our immediate friends and family that aspire to console us but simply can't understand what we're feeling. I'm thankful for those that sympathise, and I realise they ache for me, but there's a void in my soul that they cannot even come close to replenishing no matter how much they love me.

Thankfully, there is one that can bring comfort in this time of need... Only one that is the very guardian of life and now holds a life, my baby's sweet spirit, in the palm of His hand...

Jesus keep my baby safe, let her know she's loved...

I only yearn they know how deeply I love them...

I find myself pursuing what I must have done wrong. Was it something I ate? Should I have not taken that bath? Did I not engage in sufficient rest? And the account persists, but in reality, actions I condemn myself for can't possibly be valid, yet in my understanding I ought to have an explanation, anything to help try and make sense of it all. An entity to reprimand myself for…

If I discovered there was a reason, it wouldn't change the outcome in the least. I'm aware it's necessary I abandon the false condemnation I oppress myself with and do grasp it's important I cease straining to determine the notion, as this criticism only brings upon further distress. Not an easy task, yet for healing to begin, it's essential I put an end to blaming myself with or without reply.

I have miscarried three babies, three delightful little souls I long to hold in my embrace. My first experience came about unexpectedly. One day I witnessed my baby on ultrasound, little body, strong heartbeat. Elation and joy...

I considered all was progressing adequately until one morning I suddenly began to bleed. No pain, no discomfort, only all-encompassing fear. The following day after numerous tests and a hospital stay, I was home, although no longer carrying my baby and in a state of shock. I was without my little girl. And oh, how I miss her, there's not a day that proceeds that I don't think of her, ponder what could have been, recall the age she would be now and the milestone's she would be reaching.

My third miscarriage was complete almost as swiftly as my pregnancy began. I had been to the GP to have my pregnancy confirmed, (and I knew I was carrying a beauty.) Such joy filled my soul and the thrill of the months ahead played like a delightful musical as I set about my daily chores. However no sooner did my hope soar, did dread fill my vitality and she was gone... Absent, yet assuredly she too, left her impression...

And my second miscarriage, the one I really feel led to share, occurred by yet another different caution. Limited in my anticipation at the time, did I discern that God was going to use the next three weeks to take me on a journey, to broaden my faith and educate me to hold on to Him, no matter what the outcome. Equal to my little Holly and sweet Caroline, here I was pregnant with another cherished soul, whom I hoped for and was thrilled to be carrying. Yet after ultrasounds and various blood work, I was told that my pregnancy wasn't 'viable', my baby wasn't going to progress... I remember distinctly that first disclosure, the words 'threatened miscarriage' on the paperwork. I yearned for an escape; I craved an end from existence. Life was cruel and I couldn't recall anything other than the precious life that was meant to be flourishing inside of me. I showed no signs of miscarriage, I even had the beginnings of a baby bump. How could this contradiction be accurate? How do I persist from this position?

I went home and I prayed, I pleaded for a miracle. Heavenly Father, please turn this tribulation into a triumph...

Furthermore, I read the Bible and God lead me to specific Scriptures, awe-inspiring passages sustained with aspiration and love...

"Before I formed you in the womb I knew you,
And before you were born I consecrated you;
I have appointed you a prophet to the nations."
Jeremiah 1:5

"I will give you the treasures of darkness
And hidden wealth of secret places,
So that you may know that it is I,
The LORD, the God of Israel,
who calls you by your name."

Isaiah 45:3

As I was seeking the Lord, a picture of a little girl kneeling in a field came to my intellect. She had light brown, slightly wavy hair that tapered down her waist. She was wearing a helmet, but the helmet was considerably large on her. In addition, she was straining to lift a sizable and heavy sword, yet being so young, was limited in strength. (The Bible refers to 'the helmet of Salvation' and the 'sword of the Spirit' and I trust this was what the helmet and sword were representing). I perceived it was the spiritual armour meant for me that she was wearing. Although she was not capable to endure on her own goodwill, she'd clothed herself in this protection to strive to fight for herself due to me having given up hope. I knew in my heart of hearts it was essential I stood in faith to fight for her. It was my season to rise and take hold of the authority God had imparted upon me. As a soldier's leading weapon is a sword, so the Word of God was my greatest weapon, having infinitely more authority than any discouragement or fear. Here was a cause I boldly grasped was worth undertaking. Not only did my baby mean the world to me but I had the Lord with me and here was an opportunity to bring glory to His name.

Not long following, a friend emailed me. She was unaware of the affliction I was enduring; in addition, she was unknowing that I was pregnant, yet she was praying for me. She wrote that she felt God had placed a Scripture on her heart to convey to me. A passage from the book of Ephesians, in chapter six. She wrote that in particular, I needed to pay attention to verse 17. And take THE HELMET OF SALVATION, and the sword of the Spirit, which is the word of God.

Upon reading her email, I was filled with gratitude to the Lord for confirming what I believed He had shown me. There would be no room for doubt. I had an immense sense of peace that God had asked me to stand in faith for my baby. I was renewed by His strength and was encouraged in following His precise direction.

Finally, be strong in the Lord and in the strength of His might. Put on the full armor of God, so that you will be able to stand firm against the schemes of the devil. For our struggle is not against flesh and blood, but against the rulers, against the powers, against the world forces of this darkness, against the spiritual forces of wickedness in the heavenly places. Therefore, take up the full armor of God, so that you will be able to resist in the evil day, and having done everything, to stand firm. Stand firm therefore, HAVING GIRDED YOUR LOINS WITH TRUTH, *and* HAVING PUT ON THE BREASTPLATE OF RIGHTEOUSNESS, *and having shod* YOUR FEET WITH THE PREPARATION OF THE GOSPEL OF PEACE; *in addition to all, taking up the shield of faith with which you will be able to extinguish all the flaming arrows of the evil one. And take* THE HELMET OF SALVATION, *and the sword of the Spirit, which is the word of God.*

Ephesians 6:10-17

The following few weeks were variable. Fear periodically displayed its repugnant disposition, resulting in a lot of tears, but I intended to appreciate every moment I obtained carrying my child, I didn't want to deprive myself of such a gift. There was an intricate bond formed that would last for eternity and my heart overflowed with praise. I was determined to fight the good fight and my faith was strengthened. I kept claiming that my baby would be born whole, happy and complete. That she would lack in no pleasing measure.

The love I felt for my baby was overwhelming, the love Christ poured upon me, even more saturating...

Consider it all joy, my brethren, when you encounter various trials, knowing that the testing of your faith produces endurance. And let endurance have its perfect result, so that you may be perfect and complete, lacking in nothing.

James 1:2-4

It was a Sunday evening; my husband was attending a youth meeting and our four children were all tucked up in their beds. I discerned God was calling me to spend some time in His presence and so I put on my favourite worship music and sang. In that time, I believe another significant providence was brought to my regard.

It was of the same memorable little girl that had attempted to wear the armour. Her long hair glistened in the sunshine and her engaging blue eyes radiated with joy. She appeared exhilarated as she was holding a dandelion in her hands and blowing the seeds away… Her composure was that of bliss and I was captivated by her splendour. The greatest peace was thrust upon me, and I knew in that moment, no matter what may come to pass, God's purpose was greater than my comprehension and He held my baby in the palm of His hand. My daughter was of commendable perfection; deserving and ever so worthy…

I felt an urgency to discover what the symbolic meaning of the dandelion could be. I carried an unyielding prompting that what I'd encountered was more than purely an exquisite countenance from God, but it also held an exceptional connotation. I proceeded to search and uncovered information on what various flowers symbolise.

The dandelion was listed and it symbolises Christ's passion. What a remarkable analogy for such an insight as this. Christ holds a passion for my child, He loves my baby and demonstrates a deep interest in her wellbeing. He is passionate in His love for us as He diligently conveys comfort and hope in this delicate situation and grants a peace by illustrating He is watching over my child's happiness. Yes, indeed noteworthy, Christ's passion, but there is even more artistry to this impression.

My husband and I select to 'nickname' our babies whilst they're in the womb and can you surmise what we had nicknamed this treasured blessing?

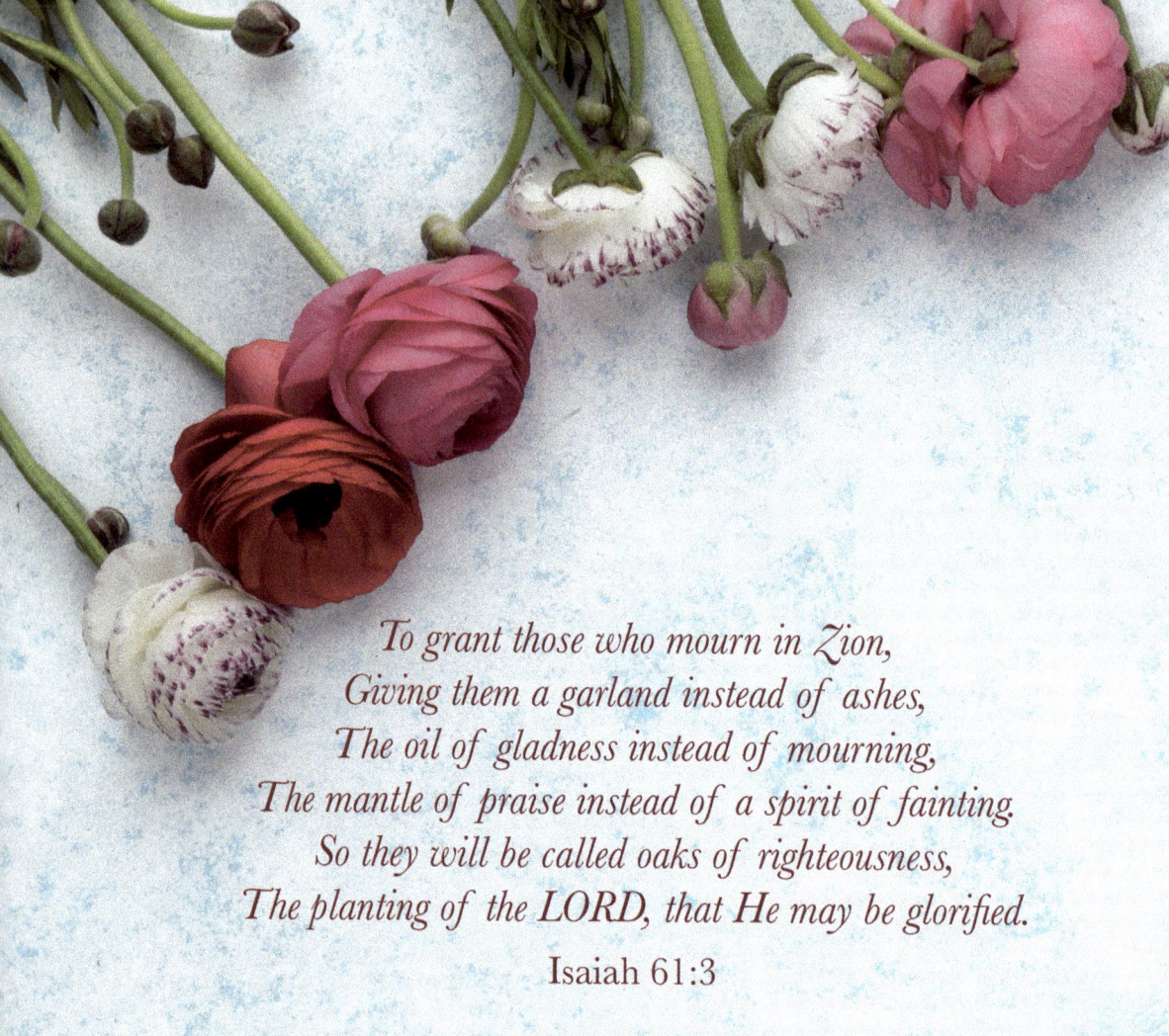

To grant those who mourn in Zion,
Giving them a garland instead of ashes,
The oil of gladness instead of mourning,
The mantle of praise instead of a spirit of fainting.
So they will be called oaks of righteousness,
The planting of the LORD, that He may be glorified.

Isaiah 61:3

Peace I leave with you; My peace I give to you; not as the world gives do I give to you. Do not let your heart be troubled, nor let it be fearful.

John 14:27

Despite the earnest prayers of mine and those close to me, my body began to show signs of miscarriage. Naturally, I was withdrawn. Grief had placed its snare upon my soul once more and I was encapsulated by the pain that pierced my heart. Nonetheless, I distinguished that I had persevered at best for my baby, that in everything there is a purpose should we choose to trust in the Almighty. Through my miscarriage, although my baby's life had been cut short here on earth, even as painful an anguish as this, I believe God will use her for something remarkable.

A couple of days following, in hospital my miscarriage ended. God calmed my spirit with His consoling breath of peace. He gave me the grace to know it was time to let go and say goodbye for now. He taught me that for a time at least, love and pain must go together. If you would know true love, then you must endure pain to because through pain, should we learn to trust and hand over our grief into His hands, returns the most valued and precious love we could ever imagine. When we experience this unblemished love, we appreciate that it's the greatest virtue to hold and it brings a striking assurance that pure love knows no boundaries. And my beautiful baby girl is now in the arms of the provider of that absolute love…

The LORD is near to the broken hearted
And saves those who are crushed in spirit.
Psalm 34:18

Grief is a process, and it requires time. It's not something that can be hurried nor avoided, and each person works through their bereavement differently. Although I'd miscarried before, it didn't make the desolation any easier to bear. Among several means I discovered it became more stringent, as not only was I grieving a second child but also reliving the unwavering memory of letting our first little treasure go.

If I could have altered the denouement, indeed I would have seized life and the liberty from sorrow. However, I was left with heartache's stain, a flaw that marred the perfection of my union with my dear child in the here and now. Still our scar too, satisfies an important role. It signifies our children shall not be forgotten and I believe our Heavenly Father with all grandeur, truly wants us to commemorate them. God can heal and furthermore diligently creates an approach for us to celebrate our esteemed children…

We may have lost the battle, but we certainly won't lose the war!

God loves 'Passiona' and I so sincerely that He uniquely used her nickname to show me He was right there in the midst of the storm. I was overwhelmed with peace and thankfulness that God had chosen to bless me ever so gracefully through a very troublesome time. I was weary, yet He restored my strength. I felt broken, yet He reached out to me in all His prestige. Because I trusted Him, even though in the natural it didn't assemble, He was able to extend my faith and demonstrate to me His unfailing love. And He aspires to bestow a crown of devotion upon you too…

Life is established the moment of conception and if God loves our children in the womb so abundantly, then wouldn't it be just to affirm that their lives certainly won't cease there?

For You formed my inward parts;
You wove me in my mother's womb.
I will give thanks to You, for I am fearfully and wonderfully made;
Wonderful are Your works,
And my soul knows it very well.
My frame was not hidden from You,
When I was made in secret,
And skillfully wrought in the depths of the earth;
Your eyes have seen my unformed substance;
And in Your book were all written
The days that were ordained for me,
When as yet there was not one of them. Psalm 139:13-16

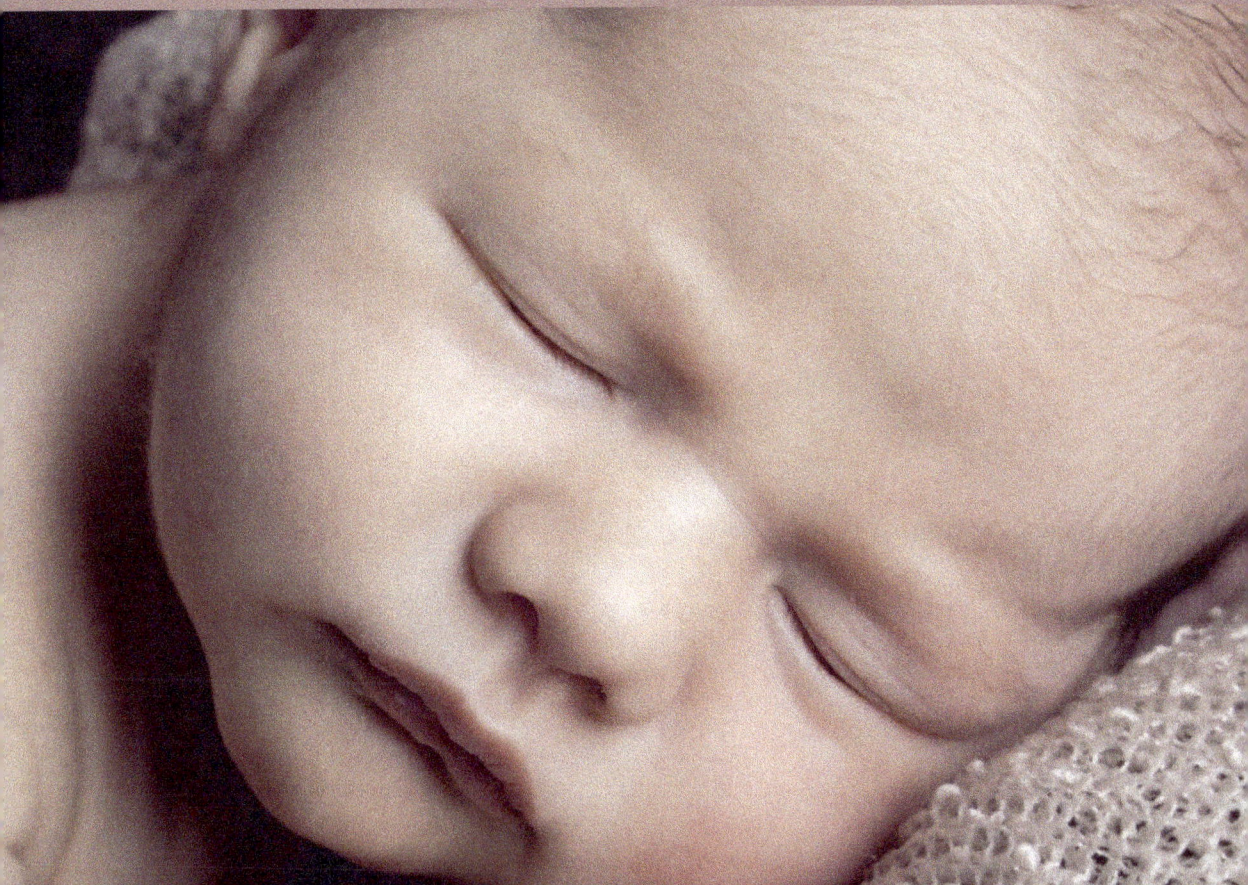

Approximately six months following my second miscarriage, I believe the Lord blessed me with His astounding assurance once more in yet another significant design. I considered how a dandelion had held a significant connotation, therefore perhaps 'holly' may as well. I proceeded in a search of the distinct shrub and was moved to tears once more by God's favour and deliberation.

Holly: Often holly is used to represent Christ's crown of thorns and therefore His passion.

More than two years preceding this discovery had God placed the name Holly on my heart and we had named our little girl. With this disclosure, I perceived our Father in Heaven connected our two daughters I miscarried long before our dear 'Passiona' was even a thought of mine or my husband's. In addition, our Caroline's middle name we chose is Rose and upon reflection, a red rose happens to symbolise passion and sacrifice. Our girls are connected and created for a valuable aspiration. This tender demonstration establishes God fastens serious thought into every child, each one of us prior to knitting us together in our mother's womb. He renders conscientious detail into every person. He knows our life story, our innermost being, before we have yet to come into existence. You my friend, are God's miracle, as is your precious child.

Heaven is a very certain place, beyond our minds comprehension but is undoubtedly present. It's a reservation so magnificent that even those with the greatest imaginations couldn't visualise to the full extent. The Bible speaks of Heaven and the Bible is truth. God is so superior and righteous, it's impossible for Him to lie.

The Bible tells us that in Heaven your child's spirit is alive and knowing. In Heaven they have freedom and safety. In Heaven our children will never experience pain, they will never estimate what it's like to feel afraid. All they will ever know is love, acceptance and perpetual bliss.

God is their devoted Father, and our children are with Him. He loves them and cares for them. They will never be lonely as everyone is together in one accord praising God with joyful delight. Oh, what a marvellous procession! And yet unlike this world, there is never a craving for another's affection as all their needs are fulfilled through their unblemished relationship with the Lord, free from the sinful disorder we currently reside in this side of glory. God does not withhold any good thing, and no one ever goes without. God is love and our children passed now rest in His perfect and abundant peace.

You will make known to me the path of life;
In Your presence is fullness of joy;
In Your right hand there are pleasures forever.
Psalm 16:11

*O magnify the LORD with me,
And let us exalt His name together.*
Psalm 34:3

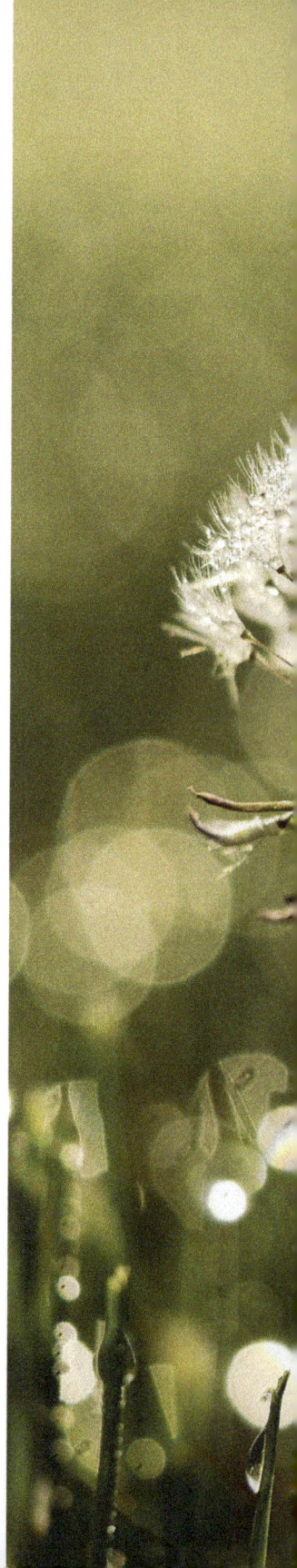

It's of great comfort to recognise your child is cherished in Heaven, that they're highly esteemed and showered with affection from the Creator of love and life Himself. You can't get any more love and adoration than the agape love of Christ.

But you ask, what about my love for my child? What about a mother's love? What about the deep longing inside my own soul to be near my baby? The immense love I have exploding from my own heart reserved for my child I've yet to even see?

There's a story in the Bible about a King who had a child, but his baby sadly died a week after being born. The circumstances here were apparent. Because King David had taken another's wife in adultery and she conceived (the wife's name was Bathsheba) and then plotted to have her husband killed and took Bathsheba as his wife himself, God commissioned the prophet Nathan to inform King David that due to his defiant acts, that the baby would die. David gave us clear indication through the following verse that we can meet with our little ones anew one day, no matter what the reason our baby passed from this place, no matter what choices we ourselves have made throughout our lifetime.

But now he has died; why should I fast? Can I bring him back again? I will go to him, but he will not return to me."

2 Samuel 12:23

We're unable to hold our babies here on earth, however a way has been made possible for us to spend eternity with them in Heaven. A place to reside with your precious one, praising God together, giving glory to our Heavenly Father for who He is and for the exuberant privilege to abide in His presence…

And the bridge into Heaven is Jesus and He's waiting only for you to ask...

Whether you believe in God or not,
He has a profound love for you,
He is with your child; holds
them in His right hand,
And He wants to carry you too...

Those whom I love, I reprove and discipline; therefore be zealous and repent. Behold, I stand at the door and knock; if anyone hears My voice and opens the door, I will come in to him and will dine with him, and he with Me.
Revelation 3:19-20

Because Jesus died on the cross, we can go to Christ and ask for forgiveness, (because we have all sinned) be washed clean and be secure knowing our names are written in the Lamb's Book of Life. When we ask Jesus to be the Lord of our life and begin a personal relationship with Him, when our lives eventually come to an end here, we progress on to live in Heaven where in turn our children reside. Through Jesus, we can meet and live forever with our beautiful children we have yet to hold. I believe without a doubt, I have three special persons that are in Heaven, and I can only imagine that first moment they can come forth to greet me, the day that I pass from this life to eternity and what a marvellous moment that will be indeed…

Inviting Jesus into your life is the foremost decision you could ever make. It's not only the doorway to Heaven to embrace your delightful child, but even greater having fellowship with Christ brings an amplitude of love and gratification into your life here on this earth. God loves us and created us to have a personal relationship with Him. Consider this, God sent His Son into the world, knowing that Jesus would have to endure affliction and hardship, His Son who is pure and blameless, yet so we could be redeemed, allowed Jesus to make the ultimate sacrifice. He didn't deserve the punishment He received; we did. Yet Jesus took it upon Himself and He did that for you…

I do not wish to delude anyone into thinking that accepting Christ is anything half-hearted. A true commitment to Christ means a person will desire to repent from their old sinful ways and begin to follow Christ. We are not perfect and life is a learning journey, but as we conform to the truth and follow Christ and His teachings laid out for us in the Bible, we become stronger, enabling us to stand firm in our faith and obedience to our Lord. As we grow in our faith, the things of this world we once felt important, tend to fade and we care more about the Lord's purposes for our lives and pursuing His will. Discipleship is costly; however, the reward of His joy truly brings more satisfaction than anything else in this world ever could.

Discipleship is costly —

Then Jesus said to His disciples, "If anyone wishes to come after Me, he must deny himself, and take up his cross and follow Me. For whoever wishes to save his life will lose it; but whoever loses his life for My sake will find it. For what will it profit a man if he gains the whole world and forfeits his soul? Or what will a man give in exchange for his soul? For the Son of Man is going to come in the glory of His Father with His angels, and WILL THEN REPAY EVERY MAN ACCORDING TO HIS DEEDS. Matthew 16:24-27

(This passage is also recorded in: Mark 8:34-38 and Luke 9:23-26)

Everyone has the right to decide for themselves if they will accept Jesus as their Saviour and if you feel that accepting Christ is something you would like to do, if you feel a stirring in your spirit, a prompting that what I am saying is for you, then I sincerely invite you to call out to Him in prayer.

Dear Lord,

I am a sinner and I ask You to please forgive me for my sins.

I acknowledge that You died on the cross and then rose again.

Thank-you for making such a great sacrifice for me.

I invite You into my heart and to be the Lord of my life.

Transform me into Your likeness, help me to live my life for You.

In Jesus name, Amen.

God never promised life on this earth would be effortless, we all go through trials in our lifetime. However, He promises to always be there for us. He will be there to comfort us in our sorrows and be our strength and shield. He will rejoice with us in the good times and with God it is certainly an exciting journey. Everything we go through; God can use for His glory. Even though at times life can be troublesome, God can bring about distinguished beauty. If I hadn't miscarried my three babies, experienced that anguish, I wouldn't have written this book. And if because I've shared my understanding with you, it has brought you comfort and peace or even better, if through reading my story, you have accepted Jesus into your life, now what greater purpose have my three daughters served than that? To Holly, Malaciah and Caroline, you have made the world a finer place, people's lives have been reformed, especially my own, because of Christ's healing through your story...

And we know that God causes all things to work together for good to those who love God, to those who are called according to His purpose. Romans 8:28

Your baby is beautiful. God created each person unique and with a monumental purpose in mind. In the case of miscarriage, we won't ever understand to the full extent 'why' but God can use all situations for good and He loves our children more than we ever could. Afterall, they are His children first.

Even grieving God has constructed. A means to release the affliction and to gently heal. If you are like me, I wanted to understand how then does God support our connection to our treasured babies whilst in the womb to be able to know a little more about them? Even in those first short weeks of life, how does He develop that intimate connection between mother and child? How can I retain any recollection of my child buried deep within my soul? The Lord created science and all the sophisticated technicalities of life He indeed fashioned together in perfect harmony. He feeds the birds of the air and clothes the flowers in thy field. Therefore, how much more will He earnestly take care of you?

Therefore, to release the pain of miscarrying a baby, I believe we first need to identify them for what they rightly are, a precious life, a human being. One with his/her own unique personality, characteristics and appearance. A human being created for good works, yet as we live in this fallen world, their life was shortened here on earth. So, by what method does God assist us to connect to the memory of our infant/s we have miscarried in order to facilitate our mourning?

All parents attach to their children and everyone who has attached to someone they lose must grieve, including babies that may not have been welcomed in the season of their conception. Approximately, 6-10 days after conception, the fertilized ovum burrows into the lining of the uterus and the placenta promptly begins its development. Through the placenta, mother and baby are intimately attached. There are simply two cells between the mother's and baby's bloodstreams. Yes, merely two. Mother and baby begin to monitor each other's emotions and blood chemistry every single moment. Our God is truly magnificent. Biologically, what is occurring in the body is recorded and reinforced in the mind. Hormones that are produced by the placenta and mother's hypothalamus affect both the thinking of the mother and her baby. Therefore, recognition of the life we were carrying, can be stored in our intellect. As the biological attachment grows, so does the attachment psychologically. Even very early losses a connection is made, as God designed humans to make these attachments. In fact, the father of our infant/s, can somehow connect too. The father all too often becomes more protective of the mother when he discovers she is with his child. This is a God given instinct. What a beautiful picture of God's safeguard for human life.

Therefore, I have discovered in my personal walk with the Lord, through prayer and if I listen attentively, I can be confident that we can bring to mind simple fragments, quiet pictures of our child to serve us to connect with the memory and therefore facilitate the grieving process to healing. Whether you spend time conversing with God regularly, I'd like to encourage you to take a moment, when it's quiet and you're on your own, to simply ask God about your baby. Even if it feels a little obscure, please give it a try, as it may unlock the door to some much-needed healing for you. Perhaps you could begin by asking the Lord the sex of your baby if your loss was too early to have determined or if you were waiting for the surprise at birth? You can ask God anything through prayer, any questions you may have. We may not receive all the answers, we may not always hear correctly, yet being able to identify our child for what they truly are, a human being, will assist our connection to the heartbreaking loss and therefore aid the all-important grieving process.

Please note, for our well-being, Scripture makes it very clear that we should never communicate with the spirit of anyone who has passed away. We humans are unable to readily distinguish between spirits. All too often evil spirits have disguised as the deceased and subsequently, causing interference in the grieving process. Therefore, I urge you to take heed and direct all your queries to the Lord alone.

We are all different and God knows you earnestly. He knows how best to converse with your heart. He is trustworthy. His greatest manner of speaking to us is through the Bible. The Bible is the living Word, sharper than a two-edged sword. It can break through bondages and bring about healing like no other consolation. Alongside the Word, He may choose to bring reassurance to you through a providence or a dream. A friend might have a word for you. There are numerous ways that God speaks, we just need to seek Him. In addition, to know with confidence something is from God, it will always line up with the Bible. When we are one with Christ, we can also rely on the Holy Spirit to guide us through discernment and grant us His peace. Again, the Holy Spirit's guidance will line up with the Bible and His peace is unlike something that simply 'feels good'.

A final instrument I found to be a major component of my healing was to name my girls and I encourage you if you consider it befitting, to also name your baby. I found great comfort in personally naming them. With Holly, my husband and I waited until her due date to name her, I wanted to be assured of the name we chose. With Malaciah and Caroline, we decided on their names not long after each miscarriage, so we named them sooner. But there is no appointed season, only if or when you are ready.

Trust in the LORD with all your heart
And do not lean on your own understanding.
In all your ways acknowledge Him,
And He will make your paths straight.
Do not be wise in your own eyes;
Fear the LORD and turn away from evil.
It will be healing to your body
And refreshment to your bones.
Proverbs 3:5-8

Holly Grace Wright

As you write by her candlelight,
Allow yourself a moment to feel,
I know how much you miss her,
And I am here to help you heal.

I know it's hard to understand,
Yet please trust I have a special reason,
I make everything beautiful in its time,
For every activity under Heaven there is a season.

From the very moment of conception,
A tiny spirit comes into being,
One I can assure you will live life to the full,
There is so much more to this than you are seeing.

She knows how much her mummy loves her,
I tell her of you all the time,
She loves to sit up on My lap,
To feel your love through Mine…

I promise you she is happy,
I guarantee she is complete,
Surrounded by only innocence and purity,
A little treasure just waiting for her family to meet.

By all means keep her memory alive there,
Through love and inner peace,
Take your time to grieve; we can work at your pace,
I love you; as does our precious Holly Grace…

Journal and reflection.

May your personal journaling bring healing and hope to your heart.

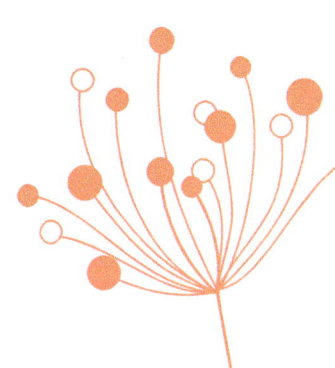

A love I long to meet

My baby gone too soon,
A love I long to meet,
My precious Holly Grace.

Your radiant eyes of blue,
And sandy golden hair,
Complement your pink blushed cheeks,
And skin that's oh so fair.

You dance before the King,
You're as happy as can be,
You walk alongside angels,
At Heavens gates you wait for me.

Safe in Jesus' arms,
A love I long to meet,
My precious Holly Grace…

The next couple of pages are arranged for you to write about how you're feeling and to write questions you may like answers too. Remember, there are no right or mistaken answers. This is for you and is your own free space. Address anything you desire about your child, perhaps what you imagine he or she may have looked like and the personality traits you find yourself anticipating your child may have acquired. Maybe you could write down the names you were contemplating choosing from for your infant. Write whatever it is on your heart to write about.

_____

_____

_____

_____

_____

_____

_____

_____

_____

Every life is beautiful...

My child's name is:

_____

Date of remembrance:

_____

*"The very moment you were conceived,
You changed my life for the better.
You're a delight to my heart and I'll never stop loving you."*

We have today...

You came into being,
A welcomed blessing within my womb,
Taylored together with joy and wonder,
A gentle excitement springing up in bloom.

Oh, the riches of your significance,
I often think back to that blissful peace,
A blink of awe inspired thrill,
A longing the Lord so gracefully filled.

All I knew was that I had today,
Right here, right now, with you,
I embraced our union; our souls entwined,
My blessing; my treasure; your heart etched in mine.

Forevermore my song of happiness,
A tender affection held close by,
A fleeting occasion, yet oh so noteworthy,
An unanswered loss and I wish I knew why...

Yet I am thankful for our moment,
I am grateful that you came,
Your memory will last my lifetime,
Caroline Rose - a beauty one and the same.

Many a time, fathers' are somewhat forsaken when it comes to miscarriage. People's concerns are primarily focused on how the mother is coping, therefore don't consider inquiring how the father is managing. In many instances, dad himself is also more worried about the distress his beloved is enduring. But it was his baby too and it's important for the fathers to have their disappointment listened to as well. Notably, everyone deals with sadness by their own measure, some people want to converse, and some people find it more fitting to deal with grief on one's own. However, I wish to affirm, to all the fathers of loss, I pray you find healing and reward through this journey. You are made in God's very image and He cares for you. Your baby would be pleased to meet you and loves you endlessly…

To all the mothers reading this, you are of exceptional value in the eyes of the Lord. You are worth more than diamonds and more precious than rubies. I know you yearn for your baby, but take heart in knowing that he/she is safe in Jesus' arms, free to abide, be blessed and cherished forever…

God cares for you, and He cares for your child. As you carry your baby in your heart, He will carry you. He is with you, understands you and loves you markedly more than you could ever imagine…

"Listen to Me, O house of Jacob,
And all the remnant of the house of Israel,
You who have been borne by Me from birth
And have been carried from the womb;
Even to your old age I will be the same,
And even to your graying years I will bear you!
I have done it, and I will carry you;
And I will bear you and I will deliver you.

Isaiah 46:3-4

I had longed to encounter a miracle, with every fraction of my being. I aspired to witness the implausible with undiminished devotion. With God, all things are possible, and He had listened attentively to my every prayer. The Lord is indeed faithful, and He answered those prayers fervently. Not by the approach I anticipated, for He had a greater plan. He answered my prayers with eternity in mind…

Our children in Heaven have a prized lesson to teach. With their innocent hearts and compassionate souls, they now rejoice in Jesus, whom we know deeply values their worth. They softly abide in the celebration of loving, simply because they know it is jubilant to love wholeheartedly…

In my heart I hold my children, they are a blessing and a joy. In my heart I also bear Christ's passion, His passion for you and our adoring babies. The cry of my affection is for those that have ever suffered the loss of a child whether through miscarriage, abortion, stillbirth, sickness or accident can know how profusely their child would delight in uniting with them in Heaven one day. And my earnest prayer is that you find peace within through Jesus Christ, the One and Only true Healer and Redeemer.

A sinner's prayer...

Dear Lord in Heaven,
I come to You this day,
To ask You for forgiveness,
In sincerity I pray.

I confess that I have sinned,
I want to start my life anew,
Please help me live a life that's pure,
And honour You in all I do.

I invite You into my life,
Please come and dwell in my heart,
Give me a longing to seek Your face,
Supply me the strength to live by Your grace.

I believe You died upon the cross,
Paid the price for my sin,
Thank you for Your unconditional love,
Thank you for the gift of eternal life above.

Today I am born again!
A new creation in Christ,
My spirit is now alive to live for You,
Jesus, be beside me in all I do.

In Jesus name, Amen.

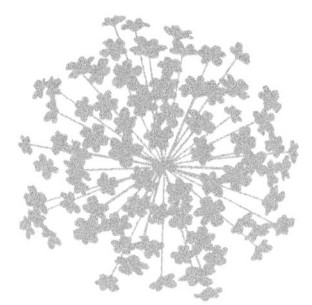

Contact the author

Thank you for reading my testimony. I trust it has been consoling for you.

For further information or to contact me, please visit:

heidelwright.com

www.ingramcontent.com/pod-product-compliance
Lightning Source LLC
LaVergne TN
LVHW070948070426
835507LV00028B/3452